PYTHON PROGRAMMING

Python Programming – A Step-by-Step Guide from Absolute Beginners to Complete Guide for intermediates and Advanced is about getting up and running fast with Python. You want to learn the language quickly to be productive when you use it to do your real work, which could be anything. Unlike most books on the subject, it starts from the beginning showing you t differences between Python and other languages. As a result, you get an understanding of what needs to be done from the beginning, using practical examples and spending a lot of time doing really useful tasks. You can also get help installing Python on your particular system.

When you have a good installation on any platform you are using, start with the basics and go up. When you finish reading the examples in this book, you will need to write simple programs and perform different tasks using Python. You can use Python to meet specific needs in the work environment.

If you are a beginner in a hurry to start using Python as quickly as possible, you can move on to Chapter 2 with the knowledge that you will find some confusing topics later. Moving on to Chapter 3 is possible if you have Python already installed, but be sure to read at least Chapter 2 to find out what assumptions have been made during the writing of this book.

Readers who have been using Python can save time by going directly to Chapter 5. If necessary, you have the choice always to go back to the previous chapters. However, it is essential to understand how each example works before moving on to the next one. Each example has lessons that are important to you, and you may lose important content if you start to miss too much information.

PYTHON PROGRAMMING

PYTHON PROGRAMMING

A STEP-BY-STEP GUIDE FROM ABSOLUTE
BEGINNERS TO COMPLETE GUIDE FOR
INTERMEDIATES AND ADVANCED

STEVEN SAMELSON

Copyright © 2019 by Steven Samelson

All rights reserved.

No part of this book may be reproduced in any form or by any electronic or mechanical means, including information storage and retrieval systems, without written permission from the author, except for the use of brief quotations in a book review.

CONTENTS

CHAPTER ONE - TALKING WITH YOUR COMPUTER   1
CHAPTER TWO - GET YOUR PYTHON COPY   7
CHAPTER THREE - INTERACTION WITH PYTHON   25
CHAPTER FOUR - WRITING YOUR FIRST PROGRAM   38
CHAPTER FIVE - STORAGE AND MODIFICATION OF INFORMATION   46
CHAPTER SIX - DECISIONS AND IMPLEMENTATION OF REPETITIVE TASKS   64
CHAPTER SEVEN - ERROR MANAGEMENT   89

CHAPTER ONE - TALKING WITH YOUR COMPUTER

Having a conversation with your computer can look like the script of a sci-fi movie. After all, Enterprise members on Star Trek have been talking to the computer regularly. The computer used to answer. However, with the rise of Siri (http://www.apple.com/ios/siri/) and other interactive software from Apple, you may not find such an incredible conversation.

Asking information from the computer is one thing, but giving it instructions is another. This chapter explains why you want to explain to your computer anything and what benefits you will get from it. You also discover the need for an appropriate language when performing this type of communication and explain why you want to use Python. However, most of this chapter is that programming is just a type of communication that looks like other forms of communication that you already have with your computer.

Thinking about the procedures you use frequently

A procedure is a set of steps to perform a task. For example, when you make toast, you can use a procedure like this:

1. Take bread and butter in the refrigerator.

2. Open the sack of bread and remove two toast.

3. Remove the lid of the toaster.

4. Place each piece of bread in its slot.

5. Press the toaster lever to start toasting bread.

6. Wait for the end of the toasting process.

7. Remove the toast from the toaster.

8. Put some toast on a plate.

9. Butter the toast.

Your procedure may differ from the one presented here, but it is unlikely that you put butter on the bread before you put it in the toaster. Of course, you need to remove the bread from the package before grilling it (placing bread, an envelope and everything else in the toaster would probably produce undesirable results). Most people never think about how to make toast. However, you use a procedure like this, even if you do not think about it.

Computers cannot perform tasks without a procedure. You must tell the computer what steps to take, the order in which to run them, and any exceptions to the rule that might cause failures. All this information (and more) appears in an application. Succinctly put, an application is a written procedure that you use to inform the computer what to do, when, and how to do it. As you have used procedures throughout your life, you only need to apply the knowledge you already have to what a computer needs to know about specific tasks.

Visualization of applications like any other procedure

A computer works as a primary school teacher in my example from the previous section. When you write an application, you write a procedure that defines a series of steps that the computer must perform to accomplish any task that you have in mind. If you leave out, the results will not be as expected. The computer does not know what you mean, or you intend to do certain tasks automatically. The only thing the computer understands is that you have provided a specific procedure and must perform this procedure.

Understand why Python is so cool

Many programming languages are available today. A student can spend an entire semester at university and study computer languages without always hearing from everyone. (That's what I did during my college years.) One would think that programmers would be satisfied with all these programming languages and would choose only one to talk to the computer, but they would continue to invent more.

Programmers continue to create new languages for a good reason. Every language has something special to offer - something that does exceptionally well. Also, as computer technology evolves, programming languages also evolve. Because creating an application relies on effective communication, many programmers are familiar with various programming languages to choose the right language for a specific task. One language may work better to obtain data from one database, and another may very well create user interface elements.

As in any other programming language, Python makes some exceptions, and you need to know what they are before you start using it. You might be surprised by the cool things you can do with Python. Knowing the strengths and weaknesses of a programming language allows you to use it better while avoiding the frustration of not using language for tasks that do not work well. The following sections help you make these kinds of decisions about Python.

Discover the reasons to use Python

Most programming languages are designed with specific goals. These goals help you define language characteristics and determine what you can do with the language. There is no way to create a programming language that does everything because people have conflicting goals and needs when designing applications. The main goal of Python was to create a programming language that would make programmers efficient and productive. With this in mind, here are the reasons why you want to use Python when creating an application:

Less application development time: Python code is typically 2 to 10 times smaller than comparable code written in languages such as C / C ++ and Java, which means you spend less time writing your application and more time using it.

Easy to Read: A programming language is like any other language - you must be able to read it to know what it does. Python language tends to be less difficult to read than code written in other languages, which means you spend less time interpreting and more time making necessary changes.

Learning time is Minimal: The creators of Python wanted to create a programming language with fewer strange rules making learning difficult. After all, programmers want to create applications and not learn obscure and difficult languages.

It is important to realize that although Python is a popular language, it is not one of the most popular languages. It currently ranks eighth on websites such as TIOBE, an organization that records usage statistics. (among others).). If you are looking for a language only to get a job, Python is a good option, but C / C ++, Java, C # or Visual Basic would be better choices. Make sure you choose a language that's right for you and meets your application development needs, but also what you want to accomplish. Python was the best programming language in 2007 and 2010 and was ranked the fourth most popular language in February 2011. So, it's a good choice if you're searching for a job, but not necessarily the best choice. However, you may be astonished to discover that many colleges are now using python to teach coding, which has become the most popular language at this location.

COMPARE PYTHON WITH OTHER LANGUAGES

Comparing two languages can be dangerous, because choosing a language is a matter of taste and personal preference, as is a quantifiable scientific fact. Therefore, before being attacked by the rabid protectors of the languages that follow, it is important to realize that I also use several languages and that I discover at least some degree of overlap between them. There is not the best language in the world, just the language that is best for a specific application.

C

Many people claim that Microsoft copied Java to create C #. That said, C # has some advantages (and disadvantages) compared to Java. The main (undisputed) intention behind C # is to create a better kind of C / C ++ language - a language easier to learn and use. However, we are here to talk about C # and Python. Compared to C #, Python has the following advantages:

• much easier to learn

• Smaller code (more concise)

• Fully supported as open source

• Better multiplatform support

• Easily allows the use of multiple development environments

• Easier to extend with Java and C / C ++

• Improved scientific and technical support

. . .

Java

For years, programmers have been looking for a language they could use to write an application once and run it anywhere. Java is designed to work properly on all platforms. He has some tips that you will find later in the book to achieve this magic. For now, you should know that Java has been so successful everywhere that other languages have tried to imitate it (with more or less success). Even in this case, Python has significant advantages over Java, as shown in the following list:

• much easier to learn

• Smaller code (more concise)

• Improved variables (storage boxes in the computer's memory) that can hold different types of data depending on the needs of the application during execution (dynamic typing).

• Development time is faster.

Perl

PERL originally stands for Practical Extraction and Report Language. Today, people call him Perl and let him go. However, Perl still has its roots in that it excels at getting data from a database and presenting it as a report. Of course, Perl has been expanded to do a lot more than that - you can use it to write all kinds of applications. (I even used this for a web service application.) Compared to Python, you'll find that Python has the following advantages over Perl:

• Easier to learn

• Easier to read

• Enhanced data protection

• Enhanced Java integration

• Less bias specific to the platform

CHAPTER TWO - GET YOUR PYTHON COPY

To create applications, you need another application unless you want to get a low level and write applications in machine code - a tough experience that even real programmers avoid as much as possible. Writing an application using the Python programming language requires some necessary applications. These applications allow you to work with Python by creating Python code, providing the necessary help information, and allowing you to execute the code you are writing. This chapter helps you get a copy of the Python application, install it on your hard drive, look for installed applications so you can use them, and test your installation to see how it works.

Download the version you need

Each platform (a combination of hardware and operating system software) is governed by special rules when running applications. The Python application hides these details. You enter the code that runs on any platform supported by Python, and Python applications translate that code into something that the platform can understand. However, for the translation to take place, you must have a version of

Python that works on your specific platform. Python supports these platforms:

- Amiga Research OS (AROS)
- IBM Advanced Unix (AIX)
- 400 Application System (AS / 400)
- Hewlett-Packard Unix (HP-UX)
- BeOS
- Linux

Microsoft Disk operating system (MS-DOS)

- Mac OS X (pre-installed with the operating system)
- MorphOS
- OS 390 (OS / 390) and z / OS
- Operating system 2 (OS / 2)
- PalmOS
- Psion
- playground
- QNX
- series 60
- Windows CE / Pocket PC
- RISC OS (originally Acorn)
- Solaris
- 32-bit Windows (XP and later)
- Virtual memory system (VMS)
- 64-bit Windows

Wow, that's a lot of different platforms! This book has been tested with Windows, Mac OS X, and Linux platforms. However, the examples can also work with these other platforms because they do not depend on any code specific to that platform.

To get the correct version for your platform, you need to access HTTP: // www. python.org/download/releases/3.3.4/. Since the download section is initially hidden, you must scroll down the page.

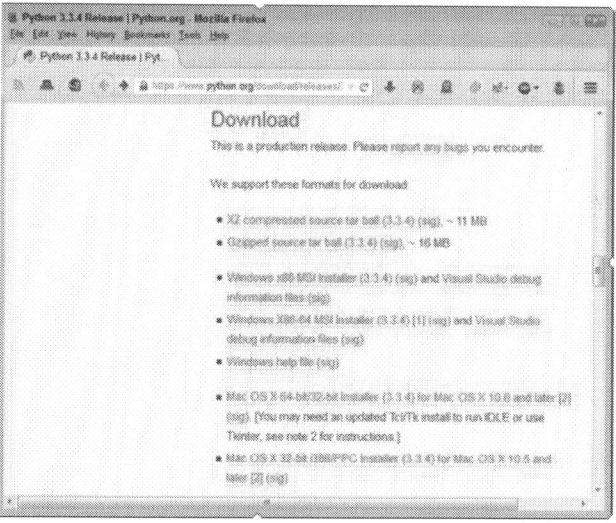

If you want to use another platform, click the second link on the left side of the page. You discover a list of Python installations for other platforms. Many of these installations are run by volunteers and not by people who create Python versions for Windows, Mac OS X, and Linux. Be sure to contact these people when you have questions about the installation, as they know how to help you get a good setup on your platform.

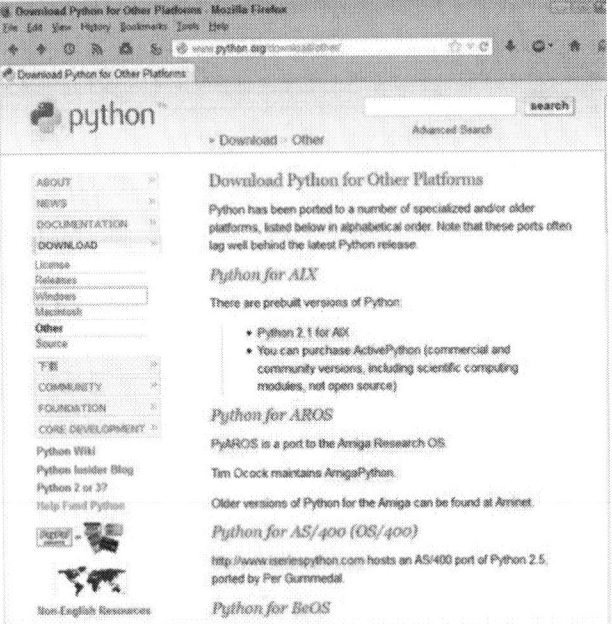

Install Python

After downloading your copy of Python, it's time to install it on your system.

The downloaded file contains everything you need to get started:

• Python interpreter

• Help files (documentation)

• Command Line Access

• IDLE (Integrated Development Environment) application

• Uninstaller (only on platforms that need it)

Work with Windows

The process of installation on a Windows system follows the same procedure that is used for other types of applications. The main difference is finding the file you downloaded so that you can start the installation process. The following procedure should work correctly on any Windows system, whether you use the 32-bit or 64-bit version of Python.

Find the downloaded copy of Python on your system.

The name of this file varies, but it usually appears under the following names: python-3.3.4.amd64.msi for 64-bit systems and python-3.3.4.msi for 32-bit systems. The version number is inserted in the file name. In this case, the file name refers to version 3.3.4, which is the version used for this book.

Double-click on the installation file.

(You can see an Open File - Security Warning dialog box asking if you want to run this file.) Click Run if this dialog box appears.) A Python Setup dialog box similar to that shown in Figure 2 is displayed. 3 The precise dialog box you see depends on the version of the Python installer you download.

Choose a user installation option, and then click Next.

The installation prompts you for the name of an installation directory for Python. Using the default destination will save you effort and time later. However, you can install Python anywhere.

Using the Windows \ Program Files (x86) folder or Program Files is problematic for two reasons. First, the folder name has space, which makes access difficult from the application. Second, the folder usually requires administrator access. You will have to constantly fight with the Windows User Account Control (UAC) feature if you install Python in any folder.

. . .

Type a destination folder name, if needed, and then click Next. Python asks you to customize your installation.

Enabling the Add python.exe option to the path will save you time. This feature allows you to access Python from the command prompt window. Do not worry too much about how you use this feature at the moment, but it's a good feature to install. The book assumes that you have enabled this feature. Do not worry about the other features you see in Figure 2-5. They are all enabled by default, giving you maximum access to Python features.

(Optional) Select on the down arrow next to the Add python.exe to path option and choose the options and will be installed on the local drive.

Click Next.

You see the installation process begin. A User Account Control box may appear asking you if you want to perform the installation. If you notice this dialog box, click Yes. The installer continues, and a Setup Complete dialog box appears.

Click Finish.

Python is ready to use.

Work with Mac

Python is probably already installed on your Mac system. However, this installation usually takes a few years, regardless of the age of your system. For this book, the installation will probably work properly.

You will not test the limits of Python programming technology - you will learn how to use Python.

The latest version of OS X at the time of this publication (Mavericks, or 10.9) comes with Python 2.7, which is very useful for working with book examples.

Depending on how you use Python, you may want to update your installation at some point. Part of this process involves installing the GCC (GNU Compiler Collection) tools so that Python has access to the low-level resources you need. The following steps begin installing a new version of Python on the Mac OS X system.

Click on the link for your version of OS X:

• Python 3.3.5 Mac OS X 32-bit i386 / PPC installation program for 32-bit versions on the Power PC processor

• Python 3.3.5 Mac OS X 32-bit / 64-bit x86-64 / i386 installation program for 32-bit or 64-bit versions on Intel

The Python disk image starts to download. Be patient: downloading the disk image takes several minutes. You can easily see how long the download will take because most browsers provide a method to monitor the download process. Once the download is complete, Mac will automatically open the disk image for you.

The disk image looks like a folder. In this folder, you see several files like python.mpkg. The python.mpkg file contains the Python application. Text files contain information about the latest compilation, licenses, and annotations.

Double-click on python.mpkg.

You see a welcome dialog that informs you about this particular Python build.

. . .

Click Continue three times.

The installer displays the latest notes on Python, the license information (click Accept when asked about license information), and finally a target dialog box.

Select the volume (hard disk or other media) that you want to use to install Python, and then click Continue.

The Installation Type dialog box appears. This dialog box performs two tasks:

Click Customize to change the feature set installed on your system.

Click Change Installation Location to change the location where the installer places Python.

The book assumes you are performing a default installation and have not changed the installation location. However, you can make use of these options in case you want to use them.

Click Install.

The installer can request your administrator password. Enter the administrator username and password, if necessary, in the dialog box and click OK. You see a Python Installation dialog box. The contents of this dialog will change as the installation process progresses. This will tell you which part of Python works with the installer.

When you have successfully installed the software, you will see a Successful Setup dialog box.

Click Close.

Python software is ready to use. (You may decide to close the disk image at this junction and delete it from your system.)

Work with Linux

Python software some with some versions of Linux. For example, if you have an RPM (Red Hat Package Manager) -based distribution (such as CentOS, SUSE, Yellow Dog, Red Hat, and Fedora Core), you probably already have Python on your system, and there is nothing else for you to do.

Depending on the version of Linux that you use, the version of Python varies, and some systems do not include the Interactive Development Environment (IDE) application. If you have an earlier version of Python (version 2.5.1 or earlier), you may want to install a newer version to access IDLE. Most book exercises require the use of IDLE.

Using the default Linux installation

The default installation of Linux runs on any system. However, you must work in the terminal and enter the commands to complete it. Some of the actual commands may vary depending on the version of Linux. The information on http://docs.python.org/3/install/ provides useful tips that you can use in addition to the following procedure.

Click on the link that matches your Linux version:

Compressed source archive Python 3.3.4 (any version of Linux)

Python 3.3.3 xzip python fonts (better compression and faster download)

. . .

You will be prompt to either open or save the file, choose Save.

Python source files are being downloaded. Be patient: downloading source files take a minute or two.

Double-click on the downloaded file.

The Archive Manager window opens. Once the files are extracted, you see the Python 3.3.4 folder in the file manager window.

Double-click the Python 3.3.4 folder.

The file manager extracts the files from the Python 3.3.4 subfolder from your folder.

Open a copy of the terminal.

The terminal window is displayed. If you have never created software on your system before, you must install the basics of the compilation, SQLite and bzip2. Otherwise, the installation of Python will fail. Otherwise, you can go to step 10 to start using Python without any delay.

Press Enter after typing the following "sudo apt-get install build-essential."

Linux installs the necessary Build Essential support for creating packages (see https://packages.debian.org/squeeze/build-essential for more details).

Press Enter after typing the following "sudo apt-get install libsqlite3-dev."

The SQLite support needed by Python software for database manipulation is installed by Linux (see https://packages.debian.org/squeeze/libsqlite3-dev).

Press Enter after typing the following "sudo apt-get install libbz2-dev."

The bzip2 support required by Python software for file manipulation is installed by Linux (see https://packages.debian.org/sid/libbz2-dev for more details).

Type CD Python 3.3.5 in the Terminal window and press Enter. The terminal changes directories in the Python 3.3.5 folder of your system.

Type ./configure and press Enter.

The script starts by checking the type of system build, then performs a series of tasks depending on the system you are using. This process can take one or two minutes because there is a long list of things to check.

Type make and press Enter.

Linux runs the creation script to create the Python application software. The manufacturing process may take a minute - this depends on the processing rate of your system.

Type sudo make altinstall and press Enter.

The system may prompt you for your administrator password. Enter your password and press Enter. At this point, several tasks occur when the system installs Python on your system.

ACCESS PYTHON ON YOUR MACHINE

After installing Python on your system, you need to know where to find it. In a way, Python makes every effort to facilitate this process by performing certain tasks, such as adding the Python path to machine path information during installation. Even then, you need to know how to access the installation described in the following sections.

Using Windows

A Windows installation creates a new folder on the Start menu containing your Python installation. You can launch it by navigating through Start> All Programs> Python 3.3.5 The two items of interest in the folder when building new applications are Python (command line) and IDLE (Python GUI).

Clicking on IDLE (Python GUI) generates an interactive graphical environment When you open this environment, IDLE automatically displays certain information to make sure you have the right application open. For example, you see the version number of Python (which is 3.3.4 in this case). It also tells you what kind of system you are using to run Python.

```
Python 3.3.4 Shell
File  Edit  Shell  Debug  Options  Windows  Help
Python 3.3.4 (v3.3.4:7ff62415e426, Feb 10 2014, 18:13:51) [MSC v.1600 64 bit (AM
D64)] on win32
Type "copyright", "credits" or "license()" for more information.
>>>
```

The Python (command line) option will open a command prompt and executes the Python command. Again, the environment automatically shows information such as the host platform and the Python version.

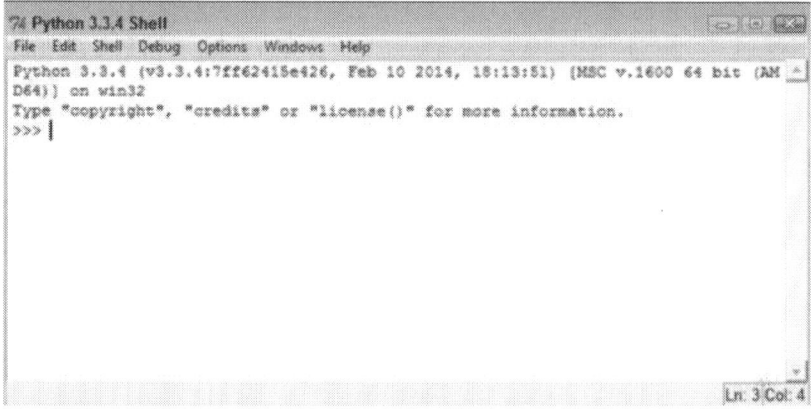

A third way to access Python is to open a command prompt, enter Python, and press Enter. You can adopt this approach when you want to gain additional flexibility over the Python environment, load items automatically, or run Python in an environment with higher privileges (in which you get additional security rights). Python provides a large set of command-line options that you can see by typing Python /? at the command prompt and press Enter. Do not worry too much about these command-line options. You will not need it for this book, but it is useful to know that they exist.

To use this third method of running Python, you must include Python in the Windows path. That's why you want to choose the Add python.exe to path option when installing Python on Windows.

This same technology allows you to add environment variables specific to Python, such as

• PYTHONSTARTUP

• PYTHONPATH

• PYTHONHOME

• PYTHONCASEOK

• PITONIOENCODING

• PYTHONFAULTHANDLER

• PATHTHASHASHED

None of these environment variables are used in the book. However, you can read more about them at http://docs.python.org/3.3/using/cmdline.html # variables-environment.

Using Mac

When working with a Mac, you probably already have Python installed and do not need to install it for this book. However, you must always know where to find Python. The following sections explain how to access Python, depending on the type of installation you perform.

Find the default installation

The default installation of OS X does not include a specific Python folder in most cases. Instead, you must open Terminal by selecting Applications⇔Utilities Terminal Terminal. As soon as the terminal is open, you can type Python and press Enter to access the Python command line version. As with Windows, using Terminal to open Python has the advantage of using command line options to change how Python works.

LOCATING THE UPDATED VERSION OF PYTHON THAT YOU HAVE INSTALLED

After running the installation on the Mac system, open the Applications folder. In this folder, you will find a Python 3.3 folder containing the following:

Pasta extras

IDLE application (GUI development)

Python Launcher (development of interactive commands)

Update Sh ...

Double-click the IDLE application to open an interactive graphical environment. There are some minor cosmetic differences, but the contents of the window are identical. Double-click the Python launcher to open a command-line environment. This environment uses all Python defaults to provide a default runtime environment.

Even if you install the latest version of Python on your Mac, you do not have to use the default environment. You can still open Terminal to access Python command-line switches. However, when you launch Python from the Mac Terminal application, you must ensure that you do not access the default installation. Don't forget to add / usr / local / bin / Python3.3.5 to your shell search path.

Use Linux

After you have successfully installed Python, you can find a Python 3.3 subfolder in your folder. The directory of Python 3.3 on your Linux system is usually the /usr/local/bin/Python3.3 folder. This information is important because you may need to change the path to your system manually. Linux developers must type Python3.3, not just Python when working in the Terminal window to access the Python 3.3.4 installation.

Test your installation

To make sure your installation is usable, you must test it. It's essential to know that your installation will work as expected when you need it. Of course, that means writing your first application in Python. To begin, open a copy of IDLE. As mentioned earlier, IDLE automatically displays the Python version and host information when you open them.

. . .

To see the work in Python, type print ("This is my first program in Python") and press Enter. Python reveals the message you just typed as shown below. The print () command displays on the screen everything you say to display. The print () command used in this book quite often displays the results of the tasks you request from Python. This is among the commands you work with often.

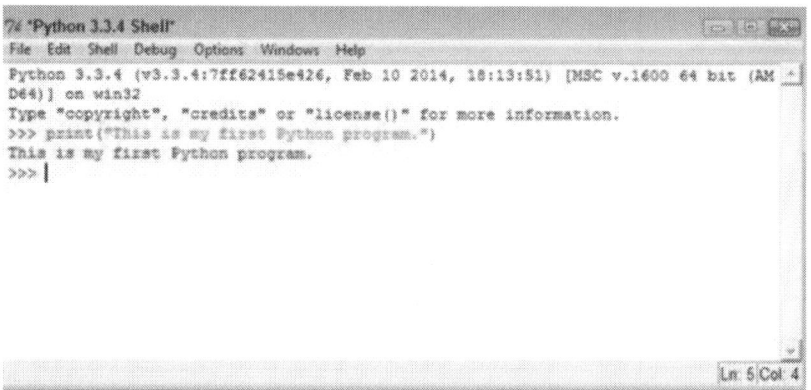

Note that the IDLE color encodes the different entries so you can see and understand them more easily. The color codes indicate that you have done well. Four color codes are shown above (although they are not visible in the printed edition of the book):

• Green: Defines the content sent to a command.

• Purple: shows that you have typed a command

• Blue: Displays the result of a command.

• Black: Define non-command entries

You know that Python is working now because you have been able to give it a command and have reacted by reacting to that command. It might be interesting to see an additional order. Enter 3 + 4 and press Enter. Python responds by issuing 7. Note that 3 + 4 appears in the black type because it is not a command. However, the seven is still in the blue type because it is produced.

```
Python 3.3.4 Shell
File Edit Shell Debug Options Windows Help
Python 3.3.4 (v3.3.4:7ff62415e426, Feb 10 2014, 18:13:51) [MSC v.1600 64 bit (AM
D64)] on win32
Type "copyright", "credits" or "license()" for more information.
>>> print("This is my first Python program.")
This is my first Python program.
>>> 3 + 4
7
>>>
                                                                    Ln: 7 Col: 4
```

Now you need to end your IDLE session: type quit () and press Enter. IDLE can display a message. Well, you don't have the intention to kill anything, but you will do it now. Click OK, and the session will be completed.

Note that the quit () command has parentheses later, just like the print () command. All commands have parentheses like these. That's how you know its orders. However, you have nothing to say to the command quit (), so leave the area between the white spaces of the theses.

CHAPTER THREE - INTERACTION WITH PYTHON

Finally, any application you build interacts with the computer and the data embedded. The focus is on data because there is no good reason to have an application without data. Any application you use manages the data in one way or another. The acronym CRUD summarizes what most applications do:

- Create

- read

- update

- Delete

If you remember CRUD, you can summarize what most applications do with your computer data (and some applications are rudimentary). However, before your application can access the computer, you must interact with a programming language that creates a to-do list in a language that the computer understands. This is the purpose of this chapter. You can interact with Python. Python takes a list of the steps you want to perform on your computer's data and changes them into bits that your computer understands.

Open the command line

Python offers several ways to interact with the underlying language. For example, you have worked a bit with the Integrated Development Environment (IDLE) in Chapter 2. IDLE makes it easy to develop complete applications. However, sometimes you want to try or run an existing application. Often, using Python's command line version works better in these cases because it allows you to control the Python environment through command-line options better, uses fewer features, and has a minimal interface.

Start Python

Depending on your platform, you can use several methods to start the command line. Here are the methods normally available:

Select the Python (command line) option in the Python 3.3 directory. This starts a command-line session that makes use of the default settings.

Open a terminal or command prompt, type Python, and press Enter. Use this option when you require more flexibility in configuring the Python environment by using command-line options.

Locate the Python directory, such as C: \ Python33 on Windows, and open the Python.exe file immediately. This option will also open a command-line session that makes use of the default settings, but you can open it with extended privileges (for applications that require access to protected resources) or change the properties of the executable file (to add command line options).

Regardless of how you start Python from the command line, you will get a prompt. If you are using a platform other than Windows, you are using IDLE instead of the Python command line version, your system is configured differently than mine, or you are using a different version of Python.) This prompt tells you the version of Python, the host operating system, and how to obtain additional information.

```
C:\Python33\python.exe
Python 3.3.4 (v3.3.4:7ff62415e426, Feb 10 2014, 18:13:51) [MSC v.1600 64 bit (AM
D64)] on win32
Type "help", "copyright", "credits" or "license" for more information.
>>>
```

Use the command line to your advantage

This section will seem a little tricky at first, and you normally do not need this information to use the book. However, this remains good information, and you will eventually need it. For now, you can search for information to find out what is available and then return to it when you need this information.

To start Python from a command prompt, type Python and press Enter. However, that's not all you can do. You can also provide additional information to change the way Python works:

Options: An option or command line option begins with a minus sign followed by one or more letters. For example, if you want help with Python, type Python -h and press Enter. You see additional information about using Python on the command line.

File Name: Providing an input file name tells Python to load that file and run it. You can run any sample application from the download code by providing the filename containing the input example. For example, suppose you have an example called SayHello.py. To run this example, type Python SayHello.py and press Enter.

Arguments: Additional information can be accepted by an application as an input to control its execution. This additional information is called an argument. Do not worry too much about the arguments now - they will appear later in the book.

Most choices do not make sense now. For example, -s is a different option from -S. Python options are

-b: Add warnings to the output when your application uses some Python features, including str (bytes_instance), str (bytearray_instance), and matching bytes or bytearray with str ().

-bb: add errors to the output when your application uses some Python features, such as str (bytes_instance), str (bytearray_ instance), and matching bytes or bytearray with str ().

-B: Do not type .py or .pyco files when you perform a module import.

-C cmd: Use the information provided by cmd to start a program. This option also tells Python to halt processing on the rest of the information as options (they are processed as part of the command).

-d: launches the debugger (used to look for errors in your application).

. . .

-E: Ignore all Python environment variables, such as PYTHONPATH, used to configure Python usage.

-h: Displays help on options and variables in the basic screen environment. Python always quits after performing this task without doing anything so that you can see the help information.

-i: Python force to let you inspect the code interactively after running a script. Force a prompt even if stdin (the default input device) does not appear to be a terminal.

-m mod: Launches the module specified by mod as a script.

-O: slightly optimizes the generated bytecode (makes it faster).

-OO: Performs additional optimization by deleting document strings.

-q: tells Python not to print version and copyright messages at the interactive start.

-s: force Python not to add the user's site directory to sys.path (a variable that tells Python where to find the modules).

-S: Do not launch "import site" at startup. Using this option means that Python will not look for paths that may contain the required modules.

. . .

-u: Allow unbuffered bitstreams for stdout (standard output) and stderr (standard error) devices. The stdin device is still buffered.

-v: Put Python in the full mode so that you can see all the import instructions. Using this option multiple times increases the level of verbosity.

-W arg: Allow Python to display small alerts by reducing the alert level. Valid arg values are

• Action

• message

• category

• module

• Lineno

-x: ignore the first line of a source code file, which allows using of non-Unix forms of #! Cmd.

-X opt: Defines an option specific to the implementation. (The documentation for your Python version discusses these options if any.)

USE PYTHON ENVIRONMENT VARIABLES TO YOUR ADVANTAGE

Environment variables are specific parameters that are part of the command line or terminal environment of the operating system. They are used to configure Python consistently. Environment variables perform many of the same options activities set when starting Python.

Most operating systems allow you to temporarily set the environment variables by configuring them during a specific session or configuring them permanently as part of the operating system configuration. How to perform this task depends on the operating system. For example, the Define command can be adopted when working with Windows.

The use of environment variables is useful when you need to configure Python in the same way on a regular basis. The Python environment variables are listed below:

PYTHONCASEOK = x: Python forces you to ignore the case when analyzing the import instructions. This is a Windows interface only for variables.

PYTHONDEBUG = x: performs the same activity as the -d option.

PYTHONDONTWRITEBYTECODE = x: performs the same activity as an option -B.

PYTHONFAULTHANDLER = x: Python forces Python tracking to fail fatally.

PYTHONHASHSEED = arg: determines the seed value that is used to generate hash values for various types of data. When this variable is at random, Python makes use of a random value to propagate the hashes of the DateTime, str and byte objects. The full valid range is from 0 to 4294967295.

Use a specific seed value to generate a predictable hash value for testing purposes.

PYTHONHOME = arg: sets the default search path used by Python to search for modules.

PYTHONINSPECT = x: performs the same activity as the -I option.

PYTHONIOENCODING = arg: specify the encoding [: errors] (such as utf-8) used for stderr, stdin and stdout devices.

PYTHONNOUSERSITE: performs the same activity as the -s option.

PYTHONOPTIMIZE = x: performs the same activity as the -O option.

PYTHONPATH = arg: provides a comma-separated list of directories (;) to search for modules.

PYTHONSTARTUP = arg: defines the file name that will be executed when the Python application is started. This environment variable doesn't have a default value.

PYTHONUNBUFFERED = x: performs the same operation as the -u option.

PYTHONVERBOSE = x: performs the same activity as the -v option.

PYTHONWARNINGS = arg: performs the same activity as the -W option.

Enter an order

After launching the Python command line version, you can begin to type commands. Using commands allows you to perform tasks, test your ideas for writing your application, and discover more information about Python. Using the command line gives you a hands-on experience of how Python works - details that can be hidden by an interactive development environment (IDE) such as IDLE. The following sections allow you to start using the command line.

Tell the computer what to do

Python, like any other programming language, depends on the commands. A command is simply a stage within a procedure. When working with Python, a command, like print (), is no different: a step within a procedure.

. . .

For the computer to know what to do, it issues one or more commands recognized by Python. Python translates these commands into instructions understood by the computer; So see the result. A command like print () can display the results on the screen for immediate results. However, Python is compatible with all types of commands, some of which show no results on the screen, but still, continue to do something important. As you move through the book, you use commands to perform all types of tasks. Each of these tasks will help you achieve a goal, as well as the steps of a procedure. When it seems that all Python commands become excessively complicated, be sure to examine them as steps in a procedure. Even human procedures sometimes become complex, but if you follow them step by step, you will begin to see how they work. The Python commands are the same. Do not be overwhelmed by them. Observe them one after the other and focus only on this step of your procedure.

Tell the computer you're done

At some point, the created procedure ends. When toasting, the process ends when you finish buttering. IT procedures work the same way. They have a point of departure and arrival. When entering commands, the endpoint of a specific step is the Enter key.

You press Enter to let the computer be aware that you are about to type the command. Throughout the book, you will know that Python offers several ways to indicate that a step, a group of steps, or even a complete application is complete. No matter how the task is done, computer programs always have a separate starting point and breakpoint.

See the result

You now know that an order is a step in a procedure and that each order has a separate start and end point. Also, command groups and entire applications also have different beginnings and endings point. So, look at how it works. The following procedure let you see the result of making use of an order:

Launch a Python file window.

An editor in which you can write the sample code is shown.

Type print ("Hello Everyone ").

Note that nothing happens. Yes, you typed an order, but this doesn't imply that the order was complete.

Press Enter.

The order is complete, and you get a result similar to the one shown below.

```
C:\Python33\python.exe
Python 3.3.4 (v3.3.4:7ff62415e426, Feb 10 2014, 18:13:51) [MSC v.1600 64 bit (AM
D64)] on win32
Type "help", "copyright", "credits" or "license" for more information.
>>> print("This is a line of text.")
This is a line of text.
>>> _
```

This exercise shows how things work in Python. Each command you type performs a task, but only after you tell Python that the command is complete one way or another. The print () command shows data on the monitor. In this case, you have provided text to display. Note that the output comes immediately after the command because it is an interactive environment in which you see the result of command immediately after it is executed by Python. Later, when you start creating applications, you realize that sometimes a result does not appear immediately because the application environment is slowing you down. Even in this case, the command is executed by Python immediately after the application informs it of its execution.

Close the command line

Finally, you want to leave Python. Yes, it's hard to believe, but there are different things to do than play Python all day. You have two standard ways to exit Python and a bunch of non-standard methods. Typically, you want to use one of the standard methods to make sure that Python behaves as expected, but non-standard methods work well when you want to play Python without doing any productive work. The two standard methods are

Exit ()

Exit ()

Each of these methods will close the interactive version of Python. The shell (the Python program) is created to take in any command.

Both commands can accept an optional argument. For instance, you can type exit (5) or quit (5), and press Enter to exit the shell. The numeric argument sets the ERRORLEVEL environment variable from the command prompt, which you can intercept as part of a batch file or on the command line. The standard practice is to use quit () or exit () when the application is working perfectly.

To see this way at work, you should

Open a command prompt or terminal. You see a warning.

Type Python and press Enter on your keyboard to start Python. You see the Python prompt.

Type quit (5) and press Enter. You are provided with the prompt again.

Type echo% ERRORLEVEL% and press Enter.

You see the error code. When working with other platforms which are different from Windows, you may need to enter something other than echo% ERRORLEVEL%. For example, you type echo $ when working with a bash script.

One of the most common non-standard output methods is to click the Close button on the terminal or command prompt. Using this approach implies that your software may not have the time to perform the necessary cleanup, which can lead to unfamiliar behavior. It's always recommended to close Python using an expected approach if you're doing something other than just browsing.

You also have access to several other commands to close the command prompt if necessary. In most cases, you do not need these special commands, so you can skip the rest of this section if you wish.

When using quit () or exit (), Python performs various tasks to make sure everything is clean and organized before the end of the session. Anyway, if you think that a session may not finish properly, you can always rely on one of these commands to close the command prompt:

sys.exit ()

os._exit ()

Both commands are only used in emergencies. The first, sys.exit (), provides special error handling features that you discovered in Chapter 9. The second, os._exit (), closes Python without performing the usual cleanup tasks. In both cases, you must import the needed operating system, module, or sys before you can use the associated command. Therefore, to make use of the sys.exit () command, you use this code:

import system

sys.exit ()

Error code when using os._exit () must be provided because this command is used only when an extreme error has happened. The request to this command will fail if you do not provide an error code. To use the os._ exit () command, you make use of this code (where the error code is 5):

import the

os._exit (5)

CHAPTER FOUR - WRITING YOUR FIRST PROGRAM

Many people see application development as a sort of magic performed by wizards called geeks who waved their keyboard to produce software of any size. However, the truth is much more commonplace.

Application development follows several processes. It's more than a strict procedure, but it's not magic. As Arthur C. Clark has already pointed out, "any sufficiently advanced technology is indistinguishable from magic." This chapter deals with the suppression of the magic of the image and the introduction of technology. When you finish this chapter, you can also develop a simple application (without using magic for that).

As with any other task, users use tools to write applications. In the case of Python, you do not need to use a tool, but its use makes the task much easier to use. In this chapter, you use a tool provided with Python, the Integrated Development Environment (IDLE). IDLE goes beyond the command line tool and makes registration to this application effortless.

. . .

UNDERSTANDING THE INTEGRATED DEVELOPMENT ENVIRONMENT (IDLE)

You can create any Python application of your choice using only a text editor. As long as the editor displays clear text instead of text formatted as a word processor, you can use it to write Python code. However, using a text editor is neither efficient nor simple. To enhance the development method, developers have created interactive development environments (IDEs). The IDE provided with Python is IDLE. However, many other IDEs can work with Python.

The features provided by the IDEs vary. That's why there are many in the market. IDLE provides a set of basic features shared by most integrated development environments. It provides the necessary features to

- Write the Python code.

- Recognize and highlight certain types of special text and keywords.

- Make simple edits (such as cut, copy, and paste) and a specific code.

- Save and open Python files.

- Browse the Python path to make it easier to find files.

- Locate and locate Python classes.

- Perform simple debugging tasks (by removing code errors).

IDLE differs from the Python command line version because you get a complete graphical interface and can perform tasks much more easily via IDLE than through the command line. Also, the command line does not offer the same functionality as IDLE. Yes, you can debug your application using the command line, but it is a difficult and error-prone process. Using IDLE is much easier and faster.

Start IDLE

You find IDLE in the folder named Python 3.3 in your system as IDLE (Python GUI). When you click or double-click this entry, you see the IDLE editor. Both lines of text contain information about the Python host and provide suggestions for commands that you can try. The precise information you see differs across platforms. Your screenshots may differ from me depending on the version of Python you are using, the platform you are using, the way you have configured IDLE and your system.

Use default commands

IDLE does not list everyone, because the assumption implies that you use the features of the IDLE GUI to simplify things. However, if you wish, you can enter help (), and press Enter to enter help mode, even if this command is not listed as one of the initial IDLE commands, as is the case for the version in the command line.

Creation of the application

It's time to write your first Python program. Your first Python Shell window will not work to create an application. So you can begin by building a new Edit window for the application. You will enter the required commands and save the file to disk.

Open a new window

The first window of the Python environment is conducive to experimentation, but you need a clean edit window to enter your first application. The Python shell window provides immediate feedback for any typed command which means it is interactive. The Edit window presents a static interface in which you can enter commands, save them, and execute them after you have entered enough commands to create an application. The two windows have distinctly different purposes.

. . .

Choose File >> New File to open a new window. A new window opens. Note that the title bar says Python 3.3.5 Untitled rather than Python 3.3.5 Shell. The "Shell" password will always be displayed in the title bar of a Python Shell window. Both windows also have individual entries in the toolbar. For example, an Edit window consists of the Run command, which you will use later to test your application.

Working with the Edit window is compared to working with any other text editor. You have access to basic commands such as Cut, Copy, and Paste. If you press Enter, the next line is moved rather than executing a command as if it were running in the Python Shell window. Indeed, the Edit window is a static environment in which you enter commands and save them for later reuse.

The Edit window also provides special commands for formatting text. The "Understanding the Use of Indentation" and "Adding Comments" sections in this chapter describe how to use the formatting features. What you are required to know now is that these formatting commands act differently from those of a standard text editor because they help you control the appearance of the code instead of the generic text. Many formatting features work automatically, so you do not have to worry about it now.

Finally, the Edit window provides access to commands that tell Python to perform the steps in the procedure that you create, one after the other. This process is called running the application. The "Running the Application" section of this chapter describes this process in more detail.

Enter the order

As in the Python shell window, you can type a command in the Edit window. To see how this works, type print (note that the Edit window provides useful information about the print () command, the information is a bit concise, so you can not understand it now. And the help provided by the edit window will be more useful. For now, the value of the word is the one you must focus on. The print () command needs a value before it can print anything that is, and you will find several different values later in the book.

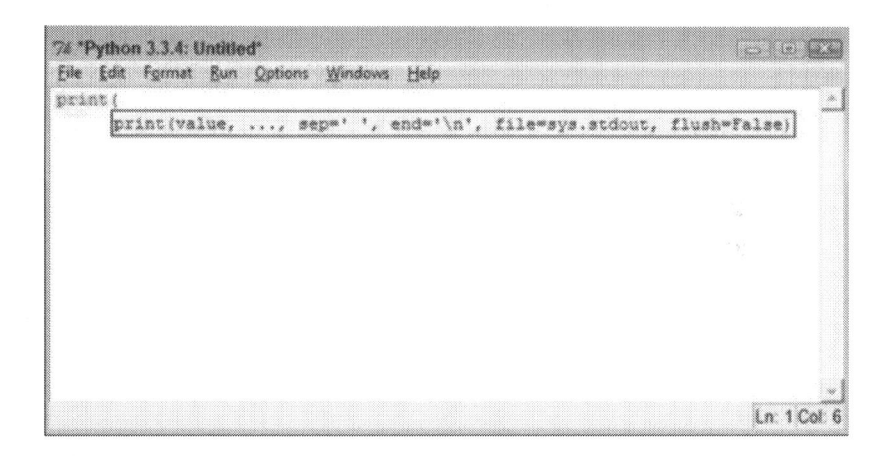

Complete the command by typing "This is a simple Python application." And pressing Enter.

Save file

You can run the application now if you wish. Nevertheless, registering your application before running it is always a good idea. For example, if you encounter an error that makes Python or the system to crash, the application code is always secure. Saving the software makes it easier to look for what did not work, make corrections, and try to rerun the application.

Choose File >> Save to display the Save As dialog box. The Python33 folder to save the application is automatically chosen by the Edit window. But, this is where the Python code resides and saving the software code in the same folder is a bad idea.

If you wish, create a directory structure with similar names using a technique that works for your platform as you follow it in the book. You can also open the source code file to download the book and avoid typing the sample code.

Type FirstApp.py in the File Name field of the Save As dialog box, and then click Save. Your application code is now saved to disk, and you can access it at any time.

When you return to the Edit window, the text in the title bar changes. Note that the title bar includes the directory to the application.

Launch the application

Applications are not very good if you can not run them. Python provides a variety of methods to run any application you create. This section explores the simplest way to run an application after it is created. It is important to recollect that Python software provides an extremely flexible environment. Thus, if one method of performing a task does not work, another method will almost certainly succeed.

To run this first application, select Run >> Run Module. You see a new copy of the Python shell window if it opens, and then the output of your application is shown.

Using comments

People take notes for themselves all the time. When you have to buy cereals, you go through your cabinets, determine what you need and write it in a list. When you arrive at the store, check your list to remember what you need. Note taking is useful for all sorts of needs, such as following the course of a conversation between trading partners or reproducing the essence of a conversation. Humans need notes to move their memories. Comments in the source code are just another form of observation. You add them to the code to remind you which task the code will be executed later. The following sections describe the comments in more detail.

Loading and running existing applications

Running your application immediately after your recording is fun and interesting, but at some point, you close IDLE and have a file on disk. The file contains your application, but you must know how to use this file to run it. Python provides a considerable number of ways to accomplish this task. The following sections describe only three of these approaches.

Using the command line or terminal window

The command line or terminal window provides a way to execute commands by typing them. You can also create batch files to run multiple commands as part of a batch process. In this case, you see the native command environment provided by the platform you are using and not the Python expert command line. You type commands to start Python and perform specific tasks when working in this environment. For example, if you want to run FirstApp, type python FirstApp.py and press Enter. You can also run any other application that way.

CHAPTER FIVE - STORAGE AND MODIFICATION OF INFORMATION

Display variables such as storage boxes

When working with applications, information is stored in variables. A variable is a type of storage container. You can access it by using the variable whenever you want to make use of the information. If you decide to store new information, put it in a variable. Changing information means first accessing the variable and then storing the new value in the variable. Just as you store objects in boxes in the real world, you store objects in variables (a type of storage box) when working with applications.

The computers are very well organized. Each variable stores only information. Using this technique, it is easy to locate the specific information you need - unlike the closet, where elements of ancient Egypt might be hidden. Although the examples you work within previous chapters do not use variables, most applications rely heavily on variables to make it easier to work with the information.

Use the correct box to store the data

People tend to store data in the wrong box. For example, you can find a pair of shoes in a socks bag and a supply of pens in a shoe box. However, Python likes to be cool. As a result, numbers are stored in a variable type and text stored in a completely different type of variable. Yes, you make use of variables in both cases, but the variable is designed to store a specific type of information. The use of specialized variables makes it possible to work with private information in a specific way. You do not need to disturb yourself about details - keep in mind that each type of information is stored in a distinctive type of variable.

Python uses specialized variables in storing data to make it easier for the programmer to keep that information secure. However, computers don't know the types of information. The computer knows only the 0's and the 1's, that is, the absence or presence of a voltage. At a higher level, computers work with numbers, but that's what computers do. The numbers, letters, dates, times, and any other type of information you can imagine are all 0's and 1's in the computer system. For example, the letter B is currently stored under the number 01000001 or number 65. The computer has no idea of the letter B, or a date is 31/08/2014.

Defining essential Python data types

Each programming language describes variables containing specific types of information, and Python is no exception. The specific type of variable is called the data type. Knowing the variable data type is vital because it tells you what kind of information you find there. Also, when you must store information in a variable, you need a variable of the correct data type to do so. Python does not allow you to store text in a variable designed to store numeric information. This will damage the text and cause application problems. In general, you can classify Python data types like numeric, string, and Boolean, although there is no limit to how to view them.

. . .

Put the information in the variables

To attach a value to a variable, you make an assignment using the assignment (=) operator. For example, to insert the number 5 into a variable known as myVar, type myVar = 5 and press Enter at the Python prompt. Although Python does not provide you with any additional information, you can still type the name of the variable and press Enter to display the value it contains.

Understand numeric types

Humans tend to think of numbers in general terms. We see 1 and 1.0 as the same number - one of them has a decimal point. However, as far as we are concerned, the two figures are the same and we could use them indifferently. Python sees them as different types of numbers because each form requires a different type of treatment. The following sections describe the integer, complex-number classes, floating-point data types supported by Python.

Stationery

The whole is an integer. For instance, the value 1 is an integer, so an integer. On the other hand, 1.0 is not an integer; has a decent party, so it's not an integer. Integers are represented by the integer data type.

Like storage boxes, variables have capacity limits. Attempting to place a very large value in a storage box will result in an error. On most platforms, numbers between -9.223.372.036.854.775.808 and 9.223.372.036.854.775.807 can be stored as an integer (which is the maximum value that can be inserted into a 64-bit variable). Regardless of how important the number is, it is not infinite.

When working with the int data type, you have access to several interesting features. One among the features is the ability to use different digital bases:

• Base 2: Make use only 0 and 1 as numbers.

• Base 8: use numbers from 0 to 7.

• Base 10: Uses the usual digital system.

• Base 16: It is also called hexadecimal and uses numbers from 0 to 9 and letters from A to F to create 16 different possible values.

To inform Python when using bases other than Base 10, add a 0 and a special letter to the number. Here are the letters you normally use:

• b: for base 2

• o: for base 8

• x: for base 16

It is also possible to convert numeric values to other databases using the bin (), oct (), and hex () commands. So by putting everything together, you can see how to convert databases using commands.

Try the command shown in the figure to see how the different bases work. Using a different base makes things easier in many situations, and you'll find some later in the book. For now, bear in mind that integer data types support different numeric bases.

Floating point values

Any number that contains a decimal part is referred to as a floating-point value. For example, 1.5 has a decimal part, so it is referred to as a floating-point value. Many people are confused with floating point numbers and whole numbers, but the difference is easy to remember. If a number has a decimal part, it is a floating-point value. Python stores float values in the float data type.

Floating point numbers have an advantage over integer values in that you can store extremely large or incredibly small values. As with integer variables, floating-point variables have storage capacity. In their case, the maximum value a variable can hold is $\pm 1.7976931348623157 \times 10308$, and the minimum value a variable can hold is $\pm 2.2250738585072014 \times 10\text{-}308$ on most platforms.

When working with floating point values, you can assign the information to the variable in several ways. The two most commonly used methods are to use scientific notation and to provide the number directly. Using scientific notation, the number of its exponent is separated. Note that using a negative exponent gives a fractional value.

Complex numbers

You may or may not remember complex school numbers. A complex number consists of an imaginary number and a real number that is associated. Real-world uses for complex numbers include:

- electrical engineering
- fluid dynamics
- Quantum mechanics
- infographics
- dynamic systems

Complex numbers also have other uses, but this list should provide some ideas. In general, if you do not practice any of these disciplines, you will probably never find complex numbers. However, Python is one of the few programming languages which gives an internal data type to support them. As you go through the book, you will find out that Python is particularly suited to science and engineering.

The imaginary part of a complex number will always stand with a j after it. So, if you want to generate a complex number with four as the real part and three as the imaginary part, you carry out a task like this:

myComplex = 4 + 3j

If you want to see the real aspect of the variable, type myComplex. The Python prompt and press Enter. Similarly, if you like to see the imaginary part of the variable, type myComplex.imag at the Python prompt and hit Enter on your keyboard.

Understand Boolean values

It may seem incredible, but computers always give a direct answer! A computer doesn't provide "maybe" output. Every answer you receive is true or false. There is a whole mathematical branch called Boolean algebra, originally defined by George Boole (a super geek of his time), on which computers rely to make decisions. Contrary to popular belief, Boolean algebra has existed since 1854 - long before the days of computers.

When you use the Boolean value in Python, you depend on the Boolean type. A variable of this type can only contain two values: True or False. You can assign a value using the True or False keywords, or create an expression that defines a logical idea equal to true or false. For example, you can say that myBool = 1> 2, which would be False because 1 is certainly not greater than 2. You see the type of bool widely used in the book, so do not worry about understanding this concept for the time being.

. . .

Understand the strings

Of all types of data, strings are the easiest to understand by humans and not by computers. If you've read the previous chapters of this book, you've seen a lot of commonly used strings. A string is simply a collection of characters that you enclose in quotation marks. For example, myString = "Python is an excellent language." assign a string to myString.

The computer does not see the letters. Each letter you use is represented by a number in memory. For example, the letter A is number 65. To see it yourself, type ord ("A") at the Python prompt and press Enter. You see 65 out. You can convert any letter to its numeric equivalent using the ord () command.

Because the computer does not understand strings, but strings are very useful for writing applications, you sometimes have to convert a string to a digit. You can use the float () and the int () commands to perform this conversion. For instance, if you type myInt = int ("123") and press Enter at the Python prompt, create an int named myInt containing the value 123.

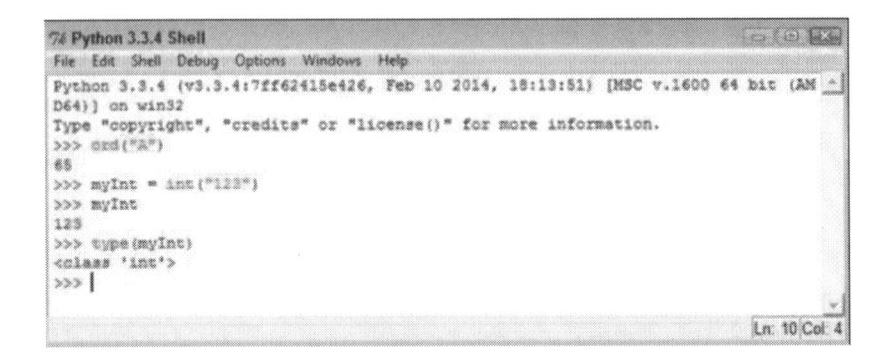

```
Python 3.3.4 Shell
File  Edit  Shell  Debug  Options  Windows  Help
Python 3.3.4 (v3.3.4:7ff62415e426, Feb 10 2014, 18:13:51) [MSC v.1600 64 bit (AM
D64)] on win32
Type "copyright", "credits" or "license()" for more information.
>>> ord("A")
65
>>> myInt = int("123")
>>> myInt
123
>>> type(myInt)
<class 'int'>
>>>
                                                                      Ln: 10 Col: 4
```

You can convert numbers to strings using the str () command. For instance, if you type myStr = str (4514.56) and press Enter, create a string with the value "4514.56" and assign it to myStr. The fact is that you can come and go between strings and numbers with ease. The following chapters show how these conversions allow for many seemingly impossible tasks.

Work with operators

Operators are the basis for controlling and managing data in applications. You use the operators to define how one data is compared to another and to modify the information in a single variable. Operators are essential to perform any math-related task and to assign data to variables in the first place.

When using an operator, you must provide a variable or expression. You are already aware that a variable is a type of storage box used to store data. An expression is a formula or an equation that describes a mathematical theory. In most cases, the output of evaluating an expression produces a Boolean value (true or false). The following sections talk about operators in detail because you use them in the rest of the book.

Define the operators

An operator accepts one or more entries as variables or expressions, performs a task (such as a comparison or addition), and then provides an output compatible with that task. Operators are classified in part according to their effect and partly according to the number of elements required. For example, a unary operator operates with a single variable or expression; a binary operator requires two.

The elements input to an operator are called operands. The operator y to the left of the operator is called the left operand, while the operator e to the right of the operator is called the right operand. The following list shows the operator categories that you use in Python:

• unary

• arithmetic

- relational

- logical

bitwise

- task

- association

- identity

Each of these categories carries out a specific task. For instance, arithmetic operators perform mathematical tasks, while relational operators perform comparisons. The following sections describe the operators according to the category in which they appear.

unary

Unary operators require only one input variable or expression. You often make use of these operators as part of a decision-making process. For example, you may want to find something else.

Arithmetic

Computers can perform complex calculations. However, the complex tasks performed by computers are usually based on much simpler mathematical tasks, such as subtraction. Python grants access to libraries that allow you to perform complex mathematical tasks, but you can still create your mathematical function libraries using simple operators.

Relational

Relational operators compare one value with another and indicate when the relationship you provided is true. For example, one is less than 2, but one is never greater than 2. The truth value of relationships is often used to make decisions in your applications to ensure that the condition to perform a particular task is met.

Logic

Logical operators integrate the true or false value of expressions or variables so that you can determine the resulting truth value. You use logical operators to create Boolean expressions to determine whether you want to perform tasks.

Gradually

Bitwise operators interact with the individual bits of a number. For example, the number 6 is 0b0110 in binary. If your binary file is a little rusty, you can use the handy converter Binary Converter in Decimal Hexadecimal at http://www.mathsisfun.com/binary-decimal-hexadecimal-converter.html. You must enable JavaScript to create the site.

A bitwise operator would interact specifically with each bit of the number. When using a bitwise logical operator, a value of 0 is considered false and a value of 1 as true.

Task

Assignment operators place data in a variable. We talked about the simple assignment operator in previous chapters of the book, but Python offers several other interesting assignment operators that you can make use of. These other assignment operators can carry out mathematical tasks during the assignment process, which allows an assignment to be combined with a mathematical operation. Table 6-6 describes the assignment operators.

. . .

Membership

Association operators detect the appearance of a value in a list or sequence and then produce the true value of that appearance. Think of association operators as if it were a search routine for a database. You input a value that you think should be present in the database and the search routine searches for it or informs you that the value does not exist in the database.

Identity

Identity operators determine whether expression or value belongs to a given class or type. You use identity operators to make sure you work with the type of information you think you are. Using identity operators can help you avoid errors in your application or determine the type of processing required by a value.

CREATING AND USING FUNCTIONS

To manage the information correctly, you must organize the tools used to perform the necessary tasks. Each line of code you create performs a specific task and combines these lines of code to achieve the desired result. Sometimes you have to repeat instructions with different data, and in some cases, your code becomes so long that it becomes difficult to keep track of what each part is doing. The functions serve as organizational tools to keep your code clean and organized. Also, the functions make it easy to reuse instructions that you have created, if necessary, with different data. This section of the chapter explains all about functions. More importantly, in this section, you start creating your first serious applications in the same way as professional developers.

Showing functions as code packages

You check your closet, open the door, and everything is spread. It's an avalanche, and you're lucky to have survived. This bowling ball on the top shelf could have done a lot of damage! However, you are armed with storage boxes, and you will soon have everything in a tidy cabinet. The shoes go in one box, the games in another and the old cards and the cards in another. Once finished, you can find what you want in the closet without fear of hurting yourself. The functions are like this: they take the messy code and put them in packages that make it easy to understand how it works and see what you have.

There are a lot of comments about their functions and why they are needed, but when you summarize the entire text, it all comes down to one idea: the functions provide a packaging code for easier location and access. If you can regard functions as organizers, you will find it much easier to work with them. For instance, you can avoid the challenge that many developers have to fill with the wrong elements of a function. All their functions will have one purpose, just like these storage boxes in the closet.

Understand the reuse of code

You go into your closet, you take off your pants and your shirt, you remove the labels, and you put them. You take everything out and throw it in the trash. Hmmm. This is not what most people do. Most people take off their clothes, wash them, and put them back in the closet for reuse. The functions are reusable too. Nobody wants to keep repeating the same task; it becomes monotonous and annoying. When you develop a function, you define a code packet that can be used repeatedly to perform the same task. All you are expected to do is invite the computer to perform a specific task telling you which function to use. The computer faithfully executes each instruction of the function, absolutely every time you request it.

When working with functions, the code that needs the services of the function is called the caller and calls the function to perform tasks. Most of the information you see about the functions relate to the caller. The caller must provide information to the caller, and the function returns information to him.

At the same time, computer programs did not include the concept of code reuse. As a result, developers had to continue to reinvent the same code. It did not take much time for someone to create the idea of functions and the concept evolved over the years until the functions became flexible enough. You can do the functions that do what you want. Reuse of the code is an essential element of

- reduce development time

- reduce programming errors

- Increase the reliability of applications

- Allow whole groups to benefit from the work of a programmer

- Make the code easier to understand

- improve the efficiency of applications

Functions make a complete list of things for applications in the form of reuse. As you go through the examples in this book, you will see how reuse makes your life a lot easier. If it were not for reuse, you would always program by manually connecting the 0s and 1s to the computer.

Define a function

Creating a role does not require a lot of work. Python tends to make things faster and easier for you. The steps below describe how to build a role that you can access later:

Open a Python shell window.

You see the familiar Python prompt.

Type def Hello (): and press Enter on your keyboard.

This step informs Python to define a function called Hello. Parentheses are important because they define the conditions of use of the function. (There is no requirement in this case.) The two dots at the end indicate to Python that you have already defined how users access the function. Note that the insertion pointer is now indented. This indentation reminds you to assign the function a task to perform.

Type this line of code: print ("My first function!"), then press Enter on your keyboard.

You should note two things. First, the insertion pointer is always indented because IDLE is waiting for you to provide the next step of the function. Secondly, Python did not execute the print () function because it is not in the main part of the window but part of a function.

Press Enter.

The function is now complete. You can tell why the insertion point is now on the left side, as shown in Figure 6-3. Also, the Python prompt (>>>) is returned.

Although this is a very simple function, it illustrates the model that you use when creating a Python function. You define a name, set the conditions required to use the function (none in this case), and define a series of steps to use the function. A function terminates when an extra line is added (you press Enter twice).

Working with functions in the Edit window means using them in the Python Shell window, with the difference that you can save the contents of the Edit window to disk. This example also appears with the source code to download as FirstFunction.py. Try to load the file into an edit window.

Access functions

After defining a function, you will probably want to use it to do useful work. This means knowing how to gain access to the function. In the early section, you create a new function called Hello (). To access this function, type Hello () and press Enter.

Each function you create will provide a similar usage model. You enter the name of the function, an open parenthesis, any required entry, and a closing parenthesis; then you press Enter on your keyboard. In this case, you don't have any input, so all you type is Hello ().

Sending information to functions

The FirstFunction.py example is fine because you do not have to keep typing this long string each time you want to say "Hello" (). However, it is also quite limited because you can use it to say only one thing. Functions must be flexible and allow you to do more than just one thing. Otherwise, you will end up writing many functions that vary depending on the data they use, not the features they provide. Using arguments helps you create flexible functions that can use a large amount of data.

Understand the arguments

The term argument does not mean that you will fight with the function; means that you provide information about the function to use when processing a request. Perhaps a better word for this would be the entry, but the term entry was used for many other purposes, the developers have decided to use something a little different: the argument. Although the name of an argument may not be clear, understanding what it does is relatively simple. An argument allows you to send data to the function so that the function can use it when executing a task. Making use of arguments makes your function more flexible.

The Hello () function is presently inflexible because it only prints a string. Including an argument in the function can make it much more flexible because you can send strings to the function to say what you want. To see how the arguments work, create a new function in the Python shell window (or open the Arguments01.py file from the downloadable source, see Entering URLs). This version of Hello (), Hello2 (), needs an argument:

def Hello2:

print (address)

Note that the parentheses are not empty anymore. They contain a word, address, which is the argument of Hello2 (). The Greeting argument is a variable that you can pass to print () to see it on the screen.

Sending the required arguments

You have a fresh function, Hello2 (). This function requires an argument before you can make use of it. At least that's what you've been told so far. Type Hello2 () and press Enter. You see an error message stating that Hello2 () requires an argument.

Return function information

Functions can display data directly or can return data to the caller so that the caller can do more. In some cases, a function directly displays the data and returns it to the caller, but it is more common for a function to directly display the data or return the data to the caller.

The operation of the functions depends on the type of task that the role must perform. For instance, a function that performs a math-related task is more likely to return the data to the caller than some other functions.

To reverse data to a caller, a function must include the return of the keyword, followed by the data to be returned. No limit to what you can reverse to a caller. Here are different types of data that you normally see returned by a function for a caller:

Values: Any value is satisfactory. You can return numbers, such as 2 or 4.5; strings, such as "Hello Boss!" or Boolean values, such as False or True.

Variables: The content of any variable works as well as a direct value. The caller receives all the data stored in the variable.

Expressions: Many developers make use of expressions as a shortcut. For example, you can return A + B instead of performing the calculation, put the result in a variable, and later return the variable to the caller. The use of the expression is faster and accomplishes the same task.

Results of other functions: You can send data from another function as part of the return of your function.

It's time to see how the return values work. Open a Python shell window and enter the following code (or open the ReturnValue.py file):

def DoAdd (Value1, Value2):

Return value1 + value2

This function accepts two input values and returns the sum of these two values. Yes, you can probably do this without using a function, but that's the number of functions started. To perform a test on this function, type print ("The sum of 4 + 5 is", do DoAdd (4, 5)) and press Enter.

CHAPTER SIX - DECISIONS AND IMPLEMENTATION OF REPETITIVE TASKS

The ability to make a decision, to follow a path or another, is an essential part of useful work. Mathematics gives the computer the ability to obtain useful information. Decision making makes it possible to do something with the information once obtained. Without the ability to make decisions, a computer would be useless. Therefore, any language you use will include the ability to make decisions in one way or another. This chapter explores the techniques used by Python to make decisions.

Think about the process you use to make a decision. You get the real value of something, compare it to the desired value, and act accordingly. For example, when you see the light and see that it is red, you compare the red light to the green light that you want, decide that the light is not green, and then to. Many individuals do not review the process they use because they use it so often every day. Decision making is natural for humans, but computers must perform the following tasks each time:

- Get the current or current value of something.

- Compare the current or current value to the desired value.

- Perform an action corresponding to the desired comparison result.

Make simple decisions using the if statement

The if statement is the easiest way to decide Python. It simply states that if a condition is satisfied, Python must perform the following steps. The following parts explain how to make use of the if statement to make decisions under different types in Python. You may be surprised to see what this simple statement can bring you.

Understand the statement if

You use statements regularly in everyday life. For example, you might say, "If it's Wednesday, I'll eat a tuna salad for lunch." The Python instruction itself is a little less detailed but follows the same pattern. Suppose you create a variable, TestMe, and set it to a value of 7, like this:

TestMe = 7

You can then tell the computer to check a value of 7 in TestMe, like this:

if TestMe == 7:

print ("TestMe equals 7!")

Each statement if python begins, curiously, with the word if. When Python sees himself, he knows you want him to make a decision. After the word comes to a condition. A condition indicates the type of comparison you want Python to do. In a situation like this, you want Python to check if TestMe contains the value 7.

Note that the condition uses the relational equality operator, == and not the assignment operator, =. A common error encountered by developers is to use the assignment operator instead of the equality operator.

The condition always ends with two points (:). If you do not provide two points, Python does not know that the condition is complete and will continue to search for other conditions on which to base its decision. After the colon, perform all the tasks you want to perform in Python. In this case, Python displays a statement that TestMe equals 6.

Work with relational operators

How an operand on the left side of an expression compares to the operand on the right side of an expression is determined by the relational operator. Once the determination is made, it displays a true or false value that reflects the true value of the expression. For instance, 7 == 7 is true, while 7 == 8 is false. The steps below explain how to make and use an if statement. This example also appears with the download source code as SimpleIf1.py.

Launch a Python shell window.

The familiar Python prompt will be shown.

Type TestNum = 7 and press Enter.

This step assigns a value of 7 to TestMe. Note that it makes use of the assignment operator (not the equality operator).

Type if TestNum == 7: and press Enter.

This step generates an if statement that tests the value of TestNum using the equality operator. At this point, notice two features of the Python shell:

The word itself is highlighted in a different color from the rest of the statement.

The next line is automatically indented.

Type print ("TestMe is 6!") And press Enter.

Note that Python still does not execute the if statement. That goes back to the next line. The word 'print' is displayed in a special color because it is a function name. Also, the text appears in another color to indicate that it is a string value. Color coding makes it much easier to understand how Python works.

Press Enter.

Shell Python overcomes this next line and executes the if statement. Note that the output is still in another color. Because TestNum contains a value of 7, the if statement works as expected.

Make multiple comparisons using logical operators

So far, the examples have shown a single comparison. In real life, you usually have to make several comparisons to meet various requirements. For instance, when baking cookies, if the timer has been turned off and the edges are brown, it is time to remove the cookies from the oven.

To perform multiple comparisons, you create different conditions using relational operators and combine them using logical operators.

A logical operator describes how conditions can be combined. For instance, you can set x == 6 and y == 7 as two conditions to perform one or more tasks. The keyword e is a logical operator that indicates that the two conditions must be true.

Interval checking, which consists of determining whether the data falls between two values, is an important element in making your application safe and user-friendly. The following steps help you to see how to perform this task. Here, you create a file so that you can run the application multiple times. This example also appears with the download source code as SimpleIf3.py.

Launch a Python file window.

An editor where you can type the sample code is shown.

Enter the following code in the window - press Enter after each line:

Value = int (input ("choose any number which is greater than 1 but less than 20:"))

if (value> 1) and (value <= 20):

print ("You typed:", value)

The example starts with getting an input value. You have no clue what the user has typed; more is any value. Using the int () function means that the user must enter an integer (one without a decimal part). Otherwise, the application throws an exception (an error indication, Chapter 9 describes the exceptions). This first check ensures that the entry is at least the correct type.

The if statement includes two conditions. The first implies that Value must be greater than 0. You can also display this condition as Value> = 1. The second condition tells you that Value must be equal to or less than 10. Only when Value satisfies both conditions will the statement succeeds and print the value entered by the user.

Choose the Run Run module.

You see an open Python environment window with a prompt to enter a number between 1 and 10.

Enter 5 and press Enter on your keyboard.

The application concludes that the number is in the correct range and generates a message.

Repeat steps 3 and 4, but type 33 instead of 5.

The application produces nothing because the number is in the wrong range. When you enter a value outside the programmed range, the instructions in the "if" block will not be executed.

Repeat steps 3 and 4, but type 6.5 instead of 5.

Python displays an error message. Although you think that 5.5 and 5 are numbers, Python considers the first number as a floating-point number and the second as an integer.

Repeat steps 3 and 4, but type Hi instead of 5.

Python displays the same error message as before. Python does not differentiate between wrong input types. You only know that the input type is incorrect and therefore unusable.

. . .

Choose alternatives using the if ... else statement

Many of the decisions made in an application fall into a category of choice of one of two options depending on conditions. For example, when you look at a traffic light, you choose one of two options: press the accelerator to continue or press the brake to stop. The chosen option depends on the conditions. A green light indicates that you can continue through the light; A red light tells you to stop. The following sections describe how Python allows you to choose between two alternatives.

Understand the statement if ... else

With Python, you select one of two alternatives using the else clause of the if statement. A clause is an addition to a block of code that modifies its operation. Most code blocks support multiple clauses. In this case, the else clause allows you to perform an alternative task, which maximizes the relevance of the if statement. Most developers make reference to the form of the if statement that contains the else clause as the if ... else statement, with the ellipses indicating that something is happening between if and else.

Sometimes, developers encounter challenges with the if ... else statement because they didn't bear in mind that the else clause always runs when the conditions of the if statement is not met. It is important to think about the consequences of always performing a set of tasks when conditions are wrong. Sometimes this can have unintended consequences.

Launch a Python file window.

An editor in which you can type your sample code is provided.

. . .

Enter the following code in the window - press Enter after each line:

Value = int (input ("choose any number which is greater than 1 but less than 20:"))

if (value> 1) and (value <= 20):

print ("You typed:", value)

other:

print ("The value you entered is incorrect!")

As before, the sample receives an input from the user and then determines whether this entry is in the correct range. But, in this case, the else clause gives an alternative output message when the user types data outside the desired range.

Note that the else clause ends in a colon, just like the if statement. Most clauses that you use with Python instructions have two points associated with them so that Python knows when the clause is complete. If you get a coding error for your software, be sure to check for the presence of both dots if necessary.

Choose the Run Run module.

You see an open Python environment window with a prompt to enter a number between 1 and 10.

Type 5 and then press Enter.

The software will check if the number is in the correct range and generates a message.

Repeat steps 3 and 4, but type 50 instead of 5.

This time, the application sends an error message. The user now knows that the entry is outside the desired range and that he must try to enter it again.

Using the if ... elif statement in an application

You go to the restaurant and look at the menu. The restaurant offers eggs, cookies, waffles, and oatmeal for breakfast. After choosing one of the elements, the server brings it to you. Creating a menu selection requires something like a statement if ... else, but with a little more force. In this case, you make use of the elif clause to generate another set of conditions. The elif clause is a combination of a separate if statement and the else clause. The following steps describe how to make use of the if ... elif statement to create a menu. This example also appears with the download source code as IfElif.py.

Launch a Python file window.

An editor in which you can write the sample code is shown.

Enter the following code in the window - press Enter after each line:

```
print ("1. red")
print ("2. Orange")
print ("3. yellow")
print ("4. Green")
print ("5. blue")
print ("6. Violet")
Choose = int (input ("Choose your favorite color:"))
if (choose == 1):
```

```
print ("You have chosen red!")
elif (choice == 2):
print ("You have chosen Orange!")
elif (choice == 3):
print ("You have chosen yellow!")
elif (choice == 4):
print ("You have chosen green!")
elif (choice == 5):
print ("You chose blue!")
elif (choice == 6):
print ("You have chosen purple!")
other:
print ("You made an invalid choice!")
```

The example begins by displaying a menu. The user sees a list of options for the application. Then he asks the user to make a selection that he places in Choice. Using the int () function ensures that the user can not enter anything other than a number.

Once the user has made his choice, the application searches for it in the list of possible values. In each case, Choice is compared to a specific value to create a condition for that value. When the user types 1, the application displays the message "You have chosen red!". If none of the options are correct, the else clause is executed by default to inform the user that the input option is not valid.

Choose the Run Run module.

You see an open Python Shell window with the menu displayed. The application prompts you to select your favorite color.

Type 1 and press Enter.

The application displays the appropriate output message.

Repeat the 3rd and 4th steps, but type 5 instead of 1.

The application shows a different output message - the one connected with the requested color.

Repeat the 3rd and 4th steps, but type 8 instead of 1.

The application shows that you made the wrong choice.

Repeat the 3rd and 4th steps, but type red instead of 1.

The application shows the expected error message. Any application you create must be able to detect errors and incorrect entries. Chapter 9 shows how to handle errors so that they are friendly.

Using nested decision statements

The decision-making process usually takes place by levels. For example, when you go to a restaurant and choose eggs for breakfast, you make a first level decision. Now the waiter asks you what type of bread you want with your eggs. The waiter would not ask that question if you asked for pancakes. The choice of toast would, therefore, become a second-level decision. When breakfast arrives, you decide if you want to use jelly on your toast. It is a third level decision. If you have selected a type of toast that does not work well with jelly, you may not have had to make that decision. This level decision-making process, each level depending on the decision taken at the previous level, is called nesting. Developers often use grouping techniques to create applications that can make complex, multi-entry decisions. The following sections describe various types of nesting that you can use in Python to make complex decisions.

Using multiple if or else statements

The most commonly used multiple selection techniques is a combination of if statement and if ... else statements. This form of selection is often referred to as a selection tree because it resembles the branches of a tree. But here, you follow a particular path to get the desired result. The sample program in this section also appears with the source code to download as MultipleIfElse.py.

Open a Python file window.

You see an editor where you can enter the sample code.

Enter the following code in the window - press Enter after each line:

x= float (input ("Input a number within the range of 100 and 200:"))

z = float (input ("Input a number within the range of 100 and 200:"))

if (x> = 100) and (x<=200):

if (z> = 100) and (z <= 200):

print ("Your secret number is:", x * z)

other:

print ("second incorrect value!")

other:

print ("First incorrect value!")

It's just an extension of the IfElse.py example that you see in the "Using the if ... else in an application" section of the chapter. Note, however, that the indentation is different. The second if ... else statement is indented in the first if ... else statement. Indentation let Python know that this is a second-level instruction.

Choose the Run Run module.

You see an open Python environment window with a prompt to enter a number between 1 and 10.

Enter 5 and press Enter.

The shell requests another number between 1 and 10.

Enter 2 and press Enter.

The combination of the two digits is displayed in the output.

PERFORM REPETITIVE TASKS

So far, all the examples in the book have taken a series of measurements once and then stopped. Many individual tasks are repetitive. For example, your doctor may state that you need to exercise more and ask you to do 100 pumps a day. If you get up, the exercise will not bring you many benefits, and you will certainly not follow the doctor's requests. Of course, as you know exactly how many pumps you do, you can perform the task a specific number of times. Python allows the same type of repetition with the for statement.

. . .

Unfortunately, you do not always know how often to complete a task. For example, consider the need to check a stack of coins for an extremely rare coin. Take only the first piece from the top, examine it and determine if it is a rare piece that does not complete the task. Instead, you should examine each piece, looking for the rare piece. Your stack may contain more than one. Only after examining all the parts of the stack can you see that the task is complete. However, since you cannot predict how many pieces are in the stack, you do not know how often to perform the task at the beginning. You know that the task is over when the stack is gone. Python performs this type of repetition with the while statement.

Most programming languages call any repetitive sequence of events a loop. The idea is to imagine the repetition as a circle, with the code rotating and rotating the tasks until the end of the loop. Loops are an essential part of the application's elements, such as menus. Writing more modern applications without using loops would be impossible.

In some cases, you must create loops in loops. For instance, to build a multiplication table, you make use of a loop in a loop. The inner loop calculates the values of the columns and the outer loop moves between the rows. You will see this example later in the chapter, so do not worry too much to understand exactly how these things work now.

Data processing using for

The first loop code block that most developers find is the state. It is difficult to imagine the creation of a common programming language without this assertion. In this case, the loop runs a fixed number of times, and you know how many times it will run before the loop starts. Because everything concerning a for loop is known at first because loops tend to be the easiest type of loop to use. However, to use one, you need to know how many times to loop. The following parts describe the for loop in more detail.

Understand the "to."

A for loop begins with a 'to' statement. The statement describes how to loop. The Python loop works through any sequence. It does not matter if the sequence is a series of letters in a chain or elements of a collection. You can even be specific about the range of values to use by specifying the range () function. Here is a simple statement.

for the letter in "Howdy!":

The declaration begins with the keyword for. The next element is a variable that contains a single element in a sequence. In this case, the name of the variable is a letter. The keyword in informs Python that the sequence follows. In this case, the channel is the "Howdy" channel. The for statement must always terminate with a colon, as well as the statements of decision making.

Retracted under the for statement are the tasks that you want to perform in the for loop. Python considers each part of the next indented statement of the block of code that constitutes the for loop. Again, the for loop works exactly like the decision statements.

Create a "basic" loop for "

The best way to see how a loop works are to create one. In this case, the example makes use of a string for the string. The for loop processes each character of the string, in turn, until the characters are exhausted. This example also appears with the source code to download as SimpleFor.py.

Launch a Python file window.

An editor in which you can write the sample code is provided.

Enter the following code in the window - press Enter after each line:

LetterN = 1

for the letter in "Hello!":

print ("Letter", LetterN, "is", Letter)

LetterN + = 1

The example begins by initializing a variable, LetterN, to track the number of letters processed. Whenever the loop ends, LetterNum is updated to 1.

The for statement works through the string of letters in the "Howdy!" String. Put each letter, in turn, in the letter. The following code displays the current value of LetterNum and its associated character found in the letter.

Choose the Run Run module.

A Python shell window opens. The application displays the chain of letters with the letter number.

Run control with the break command

Life is often an exception to the rule. For example, you may want an assembly line to produce multiple clocks. However, at some point, the assembly line is left without any required parts. If the part is not available, the assembly line must stop at the middle of the treatment cycle. The account has not been completed, but the line must be stopped until the missing part is replenished.

Interruptions also occur on computers. You may be transmitting data from an online source in the event of a network failure and terminating the connection; the stream is temporarily dry, so the application runs out of tasks, even if the number of tasks defined is not completed.

The interrupt clause is used to interrupt a loop. However, you do not just put the pause clause in your code; you surround it with an if statement that sets the condition to pause. The statement could say something like this: If the flow is dry, leave the loop.

In this example, you discover what happens when the number reaches a certain level when processing a string. The example is somewhat invented in the interest of keeping things simple but reflects what could happen in the real world when a piece of data is too long to process (which may indicate an error condition). This example also appears with the source code to download as ForBreak.py.

Open a Python file window.

You see an editor where you can enter the sample code.

Enter the following code in the window - press Enter after each line:

Value = entry ("Enter less than 6 characters:")

LetterN = 1

for letter in value:

print ("Letter", LetterN, "is", Letter)

LetterN + = 1

if LetterN> 7:

print ("The string is too long!")

pause

This example is based on the one discovered in the previous section.

However, it allows the user to provide a variable length string. When the string has more than six characters, the application terminates.

The if statement carries the conditional code. When LetterN is greater than 7, it means that the string is too long. Note the second level of indentation which was used for the if statement. In this case, the user encounters an error message indicating that the string is too long, then pauses to end the loop.

Choose the Run Run module.

A Window of Python application Shell with a prompt requesting an entry is opened.

Type Hello and press Enter.

The application lists each character in the chain.

Repeat steps 3 and 4, but type I am too tall, instead of hello.

The application shows the expected error message and terminates the string at character 6

Control of execution with continuous instruction

Sometimes you want to check all the elements of a sequence, but you do not want to process certain elements. For example, you may decide to process all information from all cars in a database, except for brown cars. Maybe you do not need information about this particular color of the car. The interrupt clause terminates the cycle, so you can not use it in this situation. Otherwise, you will not see the remaining elements of the sequence.

The continuous clause is the alternative used by many developers. As with the break clause, the continuous clause appears in an if statement. However, rather than ending completely, processing continues with the next element in the sequence.

The following steps allow you to see how the continuation clause differs from the pause clause. In this case, the code declines to process the letter w but will process all other letters of the alphabet. This example also appears with the source code to download as ForContinue.py.

Launch a Python file window.

An editor in which you can write the sample code is shown.

Enter the following code in the window - press Enter after each line:

LetterN = 1

for the letter in "Howdy!":

if the letter = "w":

Carry on

print ("Found w, untreated.") print ("Letter", LetterN, "is", Letter) LetterN + = 1

This sample program is based on the one found in the "Creating a simple loop to another" section earlier in this book. However, this sample program adds an if statement with the continue clause in the if code block. Note the print () function that is part of the if code block. You never see this printed sequence because the iteration of the current loop ends immediately.

. . .

Choose the Run Run module.

You see an open Python Shell window. The application displays the sequence of letters with the letter number. However, note the effect of the continuous clause: the letter w is not processed.

Execution control with the else statement

Python has another loopback clause that you will not find in other languages: else. The else clause makes the execution code possible even if you do not have elements to process in a sequence. For example, you may need to tell the user that there is simply nothing to do. This is what the following example does. This example also appears with the source code to download as ForElse.py.

Launch a Python file window.

An editor in which you can write the sample code is shown.

Enter the following code in the window - press Enter after each line:

Value = entry ("Enter less than 6 characters:")

LetterNum = 1

for letter in value:

print ("Letter", LetterNum, "is", Letter)

LetterNum + = 1

other:

print ("The string is empty".)

Processing data with the while statement

You use the while statement for situations where you are not sure how much data the application will need to process. Instead of asking Python to process a fixed number of items, you make use of the while statement to inform Python to continue processing items until items are exhausted. This type of loop is used when you need to carry out tasks like streaming data from a source, like a radio station or downloading files of unknown size. Any situation in which you can not define the amount of data the application will handle from the start will be a good candidate for the while statement described in more detail in the following sections.

Understand the while statement

The while statement works with a condition and not with a string. The condition indicates that the while statement must execute a task until the condition is no longer true. For example, imagine a multi-client deli in front of the counter. The seller continues to serve customers until there are no more customers in the queue. The line can (and probably will) grow as other customers are managed. It is therefore impossible to know from the start how many customers will be served. All the seller knows is that it is important to continue serving customers until there is nothing left. Here's what a while statement might look like:

while total <510:

The declaration begins with the while keyword. He then adds a condition. In this case, a variable, total, must be less than 510 for the loop to continue. Nothing specifies the Current Total value, and the code does not define how the Total value will change. The only thing is known when Python executes the statement is that Total must be less than 510 for the loop to continue with preformatting tasks. The declaration ends with two points, and the tasks are indented under the declaration.

Because the while statement does not perform a series of tasks multiple times, it is possible to create an infinite loop, which means that the loop never ends. For example, suppose that Total is set to 0 when the loop starts and the last condition is that Total should be less than 5. If the Total value never increases, the loop will continue to run indefinitely (or at least until the end of the reading, the computer is off). Endless loops can cause all sorts of weird problems in systems, such as sluggishness and even computer hang-ups, so it's best not to encounter them. You must always generate a method for the loop to complete when you use a while loop (as opposed to the for loop, in which the end of the sequence determines the end of the loop). Therefore, when you use the while statement, you must perform three tasks:

Create the environment for the condition (for example, set Sum to 0).

Specify the condition in the while statement (such as Sum <5).

Update the condition as needed to make sure the loop ends (for example, adding Sum + = 1 to the code block while).

As with the for statement, you can change the default behavior of the while statement. You have access to modify the behavior of the while statement:

Break: Ends the current loop.

Continue: immediately finish processing the current item.

Pass: finishes processing the current element after completing the states of the if block.

Else: provides another processing technique when the conditions are not met for the loop.

Making use of the while statement in an application

You can make use of the while statement in several ways, but this first example is simple. It simply displays a number based on the initial and final conditions of a variable named Sum. The steps below allow you to create and test the sample code. This example also appears with the download source code as SimpleWhile.py.

Launch a Python file window.

An editor in which you can write the sample code is shown.

Enter the following code in the window - press Enter after each line:

Sum = 0

while Sum <5:

print (Sum)

Sum + = 1

Nesting Loop Instructions

In some cases, you can use a for or while loop to achieve the same effect. The effect is the same, but the ways work differently. In this sample code, you create a multiplication table generator by nesting a while loop in a for loop. Because you want the output to be beautiful, you also use some formatting. This example also appears with the source code to download as ForElse.py.

Launch a Python file window.

An editor in which you can write the sample code is shown.

Enter the following code in the window - press Enter after each line:

Y = 1

PYTHON PROGRAMMING

Z = 1

print ('{:> 4}. format (' '), end =' ')

for Y in the meantime (1, 11):

print ('{:> 4}. format (Y), end =' ')

impression ()

for Y in the meantime (1.11):

print ('{:> 4}. format (Y), end =' ')

while Y <= 10:

print ('{:> 4}. format (Y * Z), end =' ')

Z + = 1

impression ()

Z = 1

This example starts by creating two variables, Y and Z, to keep the row and column values of the table. Y is the row variable, and Z is the column variable.

For the table to be readable, this example must create a title at the top and another at the side. When users discover a 1 at the top and 1 at a side and follow these values as long as they intersect in the table, they can see the value of the two numbers as they are multiplied.

The first print () statement will add a space (because nothing appears in the corner of the table. The formatting declaration only creates a space of 4 characters wide and includes a space. The {:> 4 part of the code defines the size of the column. The formatting function (") determines what appears in this space. The final attribute of the print () statement changes the last character of a carriage return to a single space.

The first for loop displays numbers from 1 to 10 at the beginning of the table. The range () function builds the sequence of numbers for you. When you use the range () function, you specify the initial value, which is 1 in this case, and one more value than the final value, which is 11 in this case.

At this point, the cursor is at the end of the title line. To transfer it to the next line, the code issues a print () call without further information.

Even though the following code seems quite complex, you can find out if you look at it one line at a time. The multiplication table shows values from 1 * 1 to 10 * 10, so you need ten rows and ten columns to display the information. The instruction tells Python to create ten lines.

Look again at the header of the line. The first print call () displays the value of the line header. Of course, you must format this information, and the code uses a four-character space that ends with space, rather than a newline, to continue printing information on that line.

The while loop comes next. This loop prints the columns on an individual line. The column values are the final values of Y * Z. Again, the output is formatted to occupy four spaces. The while loop ends when Z is updated to the next value using Z + = 1.

You are now back in the loop. The print () statement ends the current line. Also, Z must be reset to 1 to be ready for the beginning of the next line, which starts at 1.

CHAPTER SEVEN - ERROR MANAGEMENT

It should not be surprising that errors occur - applications are written by humans, and humans make mistakes. Most developers call application error exceptions, which means they are the exception to the rule. Because exceptions occur in applications, you need to detect them and fix them as much as you can. Detecting and dealing with an exception is called error handling or exception handling. To correctly detect errors, you must know the sources of error and know why the errors occur first. When you detect the error, you must handle it by capturing the exception. Capturing an exception means looking at it and possibly doing something about it. Therefore, another part of this chapter deals with the discovery of exception handling in your application.

Sometimes your code detects an application error. When this happens, you must throw or raise an exception. You discover that both terms are used for the same thing, which means that your code has encountered an error that can not be manipulated, and then passed the error information to another piece of code to manipulate (interpret, process, and, with a bit of luck correct exception). In some cases, you make use of custom error message objects to convey information. Although Python has a large number of generic message objects that cover most situations, some are special. For instance, you may want to provide special support for a database application, and Python will not normally cover this event with a generic message object. It's essential to know when to control exceptions locally, when to give them to the code that requested for your code, and when to create unique exceptions so that each part of the application understands how to handle the exception - all topics covered in this chapter.

You may also need to make sure that your application normally handles an exception, even if it means terminating the application. Fortunately, Python provides the final clause, which is always executed even in case of exception. You can put code to close files or perform other essential tasks in the code block associated with this clause. Even if you do not do this task all the time, this is the last topic in the chapter.

Know why Python does not understand you

Developers are often frustrated with programming languages and computers because they seem to do everything to cause communication problems. Of course, programming languages and computers are inanimate - we do not want anything from them. Programming languages and computers do not think either; they accept what the developer has to say literally. There is a problem.

Neither the computer nor Python "will know what you mean" when entering instructions as a code. Both follow the instructions you provide to the letter and as you provide them. You may not want to tell Python to delete a data file unless an absurd condition occurs. However, if you do not clarify the conditions, Python will delete the file, whether the condition exists or not. When such an error occurs, people often say that the application contains a bug. The bugs are program errors that can be removed using a debugger. (A debugger is a unique kind of tool that allows you to pause or pause running applications, examine the contents of variables, and often dissect the application to see what makes it work.)

Errors occur in several cases when the developer makes assumptions that are not true. Of course, this includes assumptions about the user of the application, who probably does not care about the extreme level of attention you received when creating your application. The user will enter incorrect data. Again, Python will not know if the data is incorrect and will care and treat it even if its purpose is to prevent an incorrect entry. Python does not understand good or bad data concepts; It simply processes the received data according to the defined rules, which means that you need to define rules to protect users against themselves.

Python is neither proactive nor creative - these qualities only exist at the developer. When the user does something unexpected, or a network error occurs, Python does not create a solution to the problem. It only deals with the code. If you do not provide the code to handle the error, it is likely that the application will fail and fail incorrectly, possibly resulting in the transfer of all user data. Of course, the developer can not anticipate all possible error situations. This is why the most complex applications contain errors - omission errors in this case.

Some developers think they can create a code foolproof, despite the absurdity of thinking that such a code is possible. Smart developers assume that several bugs will go through the process of sorting the code, that users will continue to carry out unexpected actions, and that even the smartest developer cannot predict all error conditions possible. Always assume that your application is prone to errors that may cause exceptions. This way, you will have the necessary state of mind to make your application more reliable.

Considering the sources of errors

You can guess the possible sources of error in your application by reading tea leaves, but this is not an effective way of doing things. Mistakes fall into distinct categories that help you predict (to some extent) when and where they will occur. By thinking about these kinds as you work with your application, you are much more likely to discover potential sources of error before they occur and cause potential damage. The two main categories are

- errors that occur at a given time
- errors of a specific type

The following sections describe these two categories in more detail. The general concept is that you need to think about classifying errors to be able to locate and fix any errors in your application before they become a problem.

Sort when errors occur

Errors occur at specific times. The two main deadlines are

- compilation time
- execution time

No matter when an error occurs, your application behaves badly.

The following sections describe each period.

Compilation time

A compilation error occurs when you tell Python to run the application. Python must interpret the code and put it in a format that is understandable to the computer before it can run the application. A computer depends on the machine code specific to that processor and architecture. If the instructions you have written are poorly formed or do not contain the necessary information, Python will not be able to perform the required conversion. There is an error that you must correct before the application can run.

Fortunately, compilation errors are the easiest to detect and correct. Because the application does not run with a compilation error, the user never sees this category of error. You correct this type of error when writing your code.

The occurrence of an error during compilation should inform you that other typos or omissions may exist in the code. It is always helpful to check the code to make sure there are no other potential issues that might not appear in the build cycle.

Execution time

A runtime error occurs after Python has compiled the code you are writing and the computer has started running it. Runtime errors come in different types, and some are more difficult to detect than others. You know that you have a runtime error when the user complains of an incorrect (or at least unstable) output or when the application stops working and shows an exception dialog box.

All runtime errors do not generate an exception. Some runtime errors cause instability (the application crashes), erroneous output, or data corruption. Runtime errors may affect other applications or create unexpected damage to the platform on which the application is running. In short, run-time errors can cause problems depending on the type of error you are currently using.

Many runtime errors are caused by wrong codes. For example, you can incorrectly type the name of a variable, preventing Python from placing information in the correct variable at run time. Leaving an argument optional but necessary when calling a method can also cause problems. Here are some examples of commission errors, which are specific errors associated with your code. In general, you can find these types of errors by simply reading your code line by line to check for errors or by using a debugger.

Runtime errors can also come from external sources that are not associated with your code. For example, the user may enter incorrect information not expected by the application, causing an exception. A network error can lead to access denial to a required resource. Sometimes even the hardware has a fault that causes a non-repeatable application error. These are all examples of omission errors, from which the application can recover if your application has an interrupt code. It is essential to consider both types of runtime errors (commission errors and omissions) when creating your application.

Distinguish the types of errors

Errors can be distinguished by type, that is, by the way, they are made. Knowing the types of errors helps you know where to look in an application for potential issues. Exceptions work like some other things in life. For instance, you know that electronic devices are not running out of energy. So when you try to turn on the TV without doing anything, you can try to make sure that the power cord is inserted properly into the socket.

Understanding the types of errors helps you locate errors faster, faster, and more consistently, reducing the number of diagnostic errors. The best developers know that it's always easier to fix bugs during application development than to fix it when the app is in production because users are naturally impatient and want the bugs to be fixed immediately and correctly. Also, it is always easier to fix an error early in the development cycle than to fix it when the application is nearing completion because there is less code to check.

The thing is to know where to check. With this in mind, Python (and other programming languages) divides errors into the following types:

- synthetic
- semantics
- logical

The following parts talk about each of these types of errors in greater detail. I organized the sections in order of difficulty, starting with the easiest to find. A syntax error is usually the simplest. A logical mistake is usually the most difficult.

syntactic

Every time you make a typo, you create a syntax error. Some Python syntax errors are very easy to find because the application just does not run. The interpreter may even report the error by highlighting the incorrect code and displaying an error message. However, some syntactic errors are very difficult to find. Python is case sensitive. So you can use the wrong case for a variable in one place and find that it does not work as expected. Finding the only place where you used the wrong capitalization can be quite difficult.

Most syntactic errors occur at compile time, and the interpreter points them to you. The correction of the error is facilitated because the interpreter usually tells you what to correct and with considerable precision. Even when the interpreter does not find the problem, syntax errors prevent the application from executing correctly. Therefore, any errors that the interpreter cannot find will be displayed during the test phase. Some syntax errors should make you productive as long as you pass the appropriate application tests.

Semantics

When you create a loop that runs multiple times, you typically do not receive any error information from the application. The application will work with satisfaction because it thinks that it does everything right, but that an extra loop can cause all kinds of data errors. When you create such an error in your code, this is called a semantic error.

Semantic errors occur because the meaning of a series of steps used to perform a task is false. The result is incorrect even if the code runs exactly as it should. Semantic errors are hard to find, and sometimes you need some debugger to find them.

Logic

Some developers do not create a division between logical and semantic errors, but they are not the same. A semantic error happens when the code is essentially correct, but the implementation is wrong (for instance, looping too frequently). Logical errors happen when the developer's thinking is defective. In many cases, this type of error occurs when the developer is using a relational or logical operator incorrectly. However, logical errors can also occur in any way. For example, a developer might think that the data is still stored on the local hard disk, which means that the application might behave unusually when attempting to load data from a network drive.

Logical errors are not easy to correct because the problem is not in the actual code, but the code itself is not well defined. The thinking process that led to the creation of the code is defective. Therefore, the developer who wrote the code is less likely to find it. Intelligent developers make use of a second pair of eyes to identify logical errors. Having a formal application specification is also useful because the logic underlying the tasks performed by the application is usually subject to formal verification.

Printed in Great Britain
by Amazon